THE COUNTY DURHAM BOOK

4TH EDITION

1st Edition   1973
2nd Edition   1981
3rd Edition   1992
4th Edition   1999

Cover Photograph: Durham Cathedral and Castle, from Flass Vale.

Designed and Published by Durham County Council.
Photographic Scanning by Reprographic Services, ITRS, Durham County Council.
Printed by NB Print, Part of NB Group Ltd, Gateshead.
Bound by J.W. Braithwaite & Son Ltd.

Hardback: ISBN 1 897585 55 1
Paperback: ISBN 1 897585 56 X

THE
COUNTY
DURHAM
BOOK

Foreword

As with earlier extremely successful editions, the fourth edition of the 'County Durham Book' has been designed as a photographic representation of life in the Land of the Prince Bishops. It gives an account of life in the County and of the geography and history of the County from earliest times right through to the present and in so doing marks the close of the second millennium A.D. and the beginning of the third.

The book portrays the quality of life which is available in this richly diverse County - its beautiful countryside and fresh open moorland, its picturesque towns and villages, its glorious cathedral and impressive castles, its fine country houses, and its remarkable people. The book describes what the modern County is like as a place in which to live, work and bring up a family and how the County's economy has developed and grown following the decline of the heavy industries which emerged during the industrial revolution and enabled the County to influence the world economy. The closing years of the second millennium have indeed been notable as they witnessed the final days of coalmining and of the manufacture of iron and steel which for the last two hundred years have been so important and have changed the nature of the world irrevocably.

Events which took place here have produced a County with an intense sense of identity and a recorded history which extends back almost 1,800 years. The people of the County are proud of their heritage, and long traditions have resulted in a passionate sense of belonging to County Durham. It is the strength of character of the people of this County together with their imagination, skills and determination which have led to the County's great achievements and which I feel sure ensures the County a leading role in developments during the third millennium A.D.

I am proud to be one of the people of County Durham and part of a County which has given so much and has so much still to offer. It gives me great pleasure to be able to write this foreword to this excellent publication.

LEADER OF THE COUNTY COUNCIL

Contents

CHAPTER 1

Introduction

*R*ich in history, heritage and countryside, County Durham lies at the heart of the North East of England. The County's influence nationwide, and indeed world-wide, has been outstanding and it is a hugely attractive place to live in or visit. The purpose of this book is to enhance appreciation of the County by both residents and visitors alike.

County Durham is cradled by the beautiful North Pennine hills to the west and the North Sea to the east. Its northern and southern boundaries are equally dramatic as they are formed by the large conurbations of Tyneside, Wearside and Teesside.

The evidence of human occupation of County Durham reaches back 10,000 years - an unusual and fascinating chronicle, much of which is to be seen today recorded in the form of the County's landscape and historic buildings. Whether one's taste is for Roman, Norman, mediaeval or more recent history, there is much to enjoy in the historic sites, castles, country houses and communities of County Durham. The scenic dales and river valleys, with their lush hay meadows and pasture land, offer the visitor peaceful and tranquil surroundings and opportunity to reflect on the reasons for long occupation of this beautiful place.

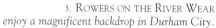

3. ROWERS ON THE RIVER WEAR
enjoy a magnificent backdrop in Durham City.

4. FIRST CLASS CRICKET
at the new Cricket Ground at Chester-le-Street.

From the seventh century onwards, the County had an important role in the development of Christianity, culminating in the building of Durham Cathedral, one of the most beautiful in Europe. During the 18th and 19th centuries, with the growth of industrialisation, County Durham made some of the most significant contributions to the world's industrial development - the birth of railways and railway engineering bear tribute to this. The 20th century has seen further great changes taking place as the heavy industries have declined and been replaced with modern industries eager to thrust forward into developments and products for the next century.

In County Durham, the past and present combine in a unique manner. With a solid foundation based on the heritage of landscape and Christian history, a growing economy based on modern and diverse industries, and the skills and strength of character of its people, the County looks forward to the opportunities afforded by the next millennium with confidence and optimism.

5. GRASSHOLME RESERVOIR *near Mickleton in Teesdale*.

6. RABY CASTLE.

Landscape

County Durham has a largely rural pattern of small villages set in surrounding countryside, and the character of its landscape is one of strong contrasts. Its 862 square miles (2,232 square kilometres) descend from the upper moors of the North Pennines through wide ridges and rolling farmland to the deep and narrow wooded valleys along the North Sea coast. Charm and natural beauty abound.

In the far west, at 2,600 feet (790 metres) above sea level, Mickle Fell represents the County's highest point. The western uplands of the County are made of limestone which was laid down in shallow seas more than 300 million years ago. 'Frosterley marble', a dark limestone in which are embedded the fossils of corals and shells, has been prized as a decorative building stone since the 13th century. It was used in the Chapel of the Nine Altars in Durham Cathedral, in the chapel of the Bishops' Palace in Bishop Auckland and in many local churches. Other geological wonders include a remarkable fossilised tree stump, thought to be 250 million years old, discovered near Edmundbyers and now displayed at Stanhope in Weardale. Petrified trees, with the cell structure still preserved, were recently found in the coal measures at Great Lumley.

COUNTY DURHAM

Landscape and Communications

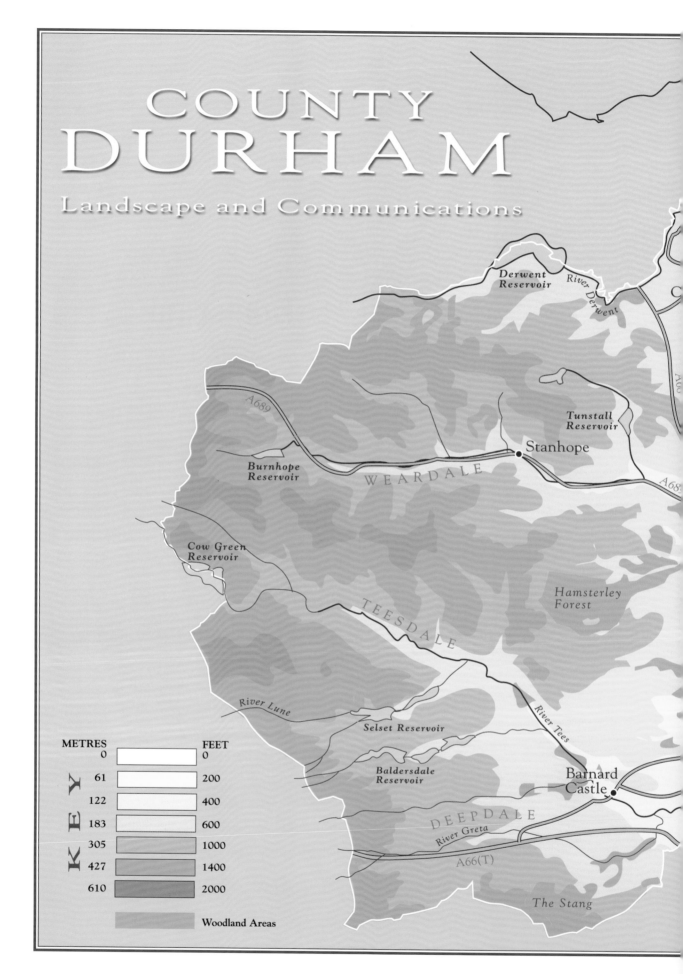

Derwent Reservoir
River Derwent
A689
Tunstall Reservoir
Burnhope Reservoir
Stanhope
WEARDALE
A68
Cow Green Reservoir
Hamsterley Forest
TEESDALE
River Lune
River Tees
Selset Reservoir
Baldersdale Reservoir
Barnard Castle
DEEPDALE
River Greta
A66(T)
The Stang

METRES		FEET
0		0
61		200
122		400
183		600
305		1000
427		1400
610		2000
	Woodland Areas	

KEY

Newcastle upon Tyne

TYNESIDE

North Sea

Sunderland

WEARSIDE

A692

A6076

Stanley

Chester
le Street

A1(M)

Seaham

A19(T)

A691

A1086

Durham
City

A690

A181

Castle Eden
Dene

Peterlee

Crook

A19(T)

Spennymoor

A177

A688

A689

Bishop
Auckland

Newton
Aycliffe

A167(T)

A1(M)

A688

A68

Middlesbrough

TEESSIDE

Darlington

River Tees

N

Kms

0   5   10

8. MICKLE FELL *in Lunedale*.

9. STANHOPE VILLAGE.

10. *Winter View Towards* CRONKLEY FELL.

11. FALCON CLINTS - *an outcrop of quartz dolerite which forms the Whin Sill.*

Here and there punctuating the limestone are huge slabs, or 'sills', of quartz dolerite. An awe - inspiring example is the Great Whin Sill at High Force in Teesdale, where the torrent of peat-brown water plunging over the rock to fall seventy feet into its basin is a magnificent spectacle. The quartz dolerite was formed deep below the earth's surface and later uplifted by earth movements and exposed to view. Further upstream, the Tees passes through Cauldron Snout, falling 200 feet in 200 yards in a series of cataracts.

12. HIGH FORCE *on the River Tees*.

13. CAULDRON SNOUT *on the River Tees*

Between Widdybank Fell and Cronkley Scar in Upper Teesdale, are 'sugar limestones', the original rock having been "baked" during periods of volcanic activity giving it its crumbly texture. Here grow rare plant species isolated since the last Ice Age, among which are Spring Gentian, Alpine Bartsia, and Birds-Eye Primrose. In the 1860s a botanist found 32 rare plant species in an area of four square miles. Over time, water at high temperatures passing through the rocks of the Pennine Dales and absorbing their chemical traces, combined with the surrounding limestone to form deposits of vein minerals such as lead and fluorspar.

14. SPRING GENTIANS
one of the rare flowers to be found in Upper Teesdale.

15. CRONKLEY FELL *a huge outcrop of quartz dolerite- an igneous rock which penetrated the carboniferous limestone of the Upper Teesdale area nearly 300 million years ago.*

16. HOLWICK FELL.

17. STANHOPE MOOR.

18. *Hill farming in* THE DURHAM DALES.

19. *Junction of the* RIVER TEES AND HARWOOD BECK *at Cronkley*.

20. *View towards* EASTGATE.

East from the watershed, peat and heather-clad moors stretch for miles and overlie thick bands of sandstone which have formed over the limestone. Here the air is especially fresh and invigorating and the countryside one of peace and solitude. Splendid isolated reservoirs lie among the upland valleys at Derwent, Burnhope, Cow Green, Selset and Balderhead. Although some are used for fishing and watersports, they too are largely oases of tranquillity.

21. *View to* GREAT DUN FELL *and* CROSS FELL *across* COW GREEN RESERVOIR.

22. GIBSON'S CAVE *near Bowlees Picnic Area.*

County Durham's three principal rivers rise as silver threads from their tributaries among the western fells. To the south, the Tees cascades over some of England's most impressive waterfalls (High Force is dramatic, Low Force, near Bowlees, more extensive) before departing the County beyond Gainford. To the north-west, the Derwent flows through upland deciduous and conifer woods and eventually joins the Tyne. In the centre, County Durham's principal river, the Wear, follows a more tortuous course east, then north, then east again, passing through and gracing many of the County's towns.

23. WATERFALL, *near Bowlees.*

24. THE RIVER TEES.

25. *Tributary of the* RIVER TEES.

26. *The County's rivers are fed by many picturesque tributaries.*

On their long journey to the sea, both Tees and Wear, aided by the passing of glaciers in the last Ice Age, have cut deeply into the landscape to create the Durham Dales. The lush hay meadows and pasture land, which clothe their sides and valley bottoms, are patterned by dry-stone walls and stone-built farms and cottages. The Durham Dales, and the moors which envelop them, form a significant part of the North Pennines Area of Outstanding Natural Beauty. Attractive small towns and villages are to be found in the valleys. In spring, daffodils brighten the village greens, and in autumn, the changing colours of the trees provide a glorious setting. In charming Teesdale, many of the farm buildings are whitewashed and stand out from the landscape, catching the sun as though highlighted by an artist.

27. *Extensive areas of the County are given over to farming.*

28. *Ox-eye daisies.*

29. *Wild flowers and dry stone wall.*

30. *Winter view to* COWGREEN *from* COWSHILL.

31. LAMBTON CASTLE.

Moving east, travelling away from the Pennines, moorland gradually gives way to a series of lower hills and valleys. In the south, the Tees valley opens out into a broad plain. This is a green and beautiful agricultural landscape dotted with attractive villages and gardens. Looking over the fields and hedges, one can admire expansive open views towards the hills of North Yorkshire. This central and gently undulating plain extends northwards through the County. It is glacial in origin, and has been the traditional artery of communication comprising the very heart of what has become known as the Land of the Prince Bishops. Impressive castles and great country houses have been built here, surrounded by parklands, and set in the green and well-kept countryside.

32. *View to* HOLWICK LODGE.

33. *Farm land in the Durham Dales.*

34. *Harvest time in Mid Durham.*

35. *Farming on USHAW MOOR.*

36. *Rich farm land under the plough.*

37. *After the harvest.*

From the eighteenth century the settlement pattern of County Durham has been strongly influenced by mining and associated industry. Few traces of coalmining can be seen today. The original beauty of the countryside has been carefully retained or restored, as traces of the damage from mining and its ancillary industries have been largely erased, as for example in the valley of the River Browney west of Durham City. The former mining and ironworking communities bring an unusual dimension to the landscape, as do the often isolated terraces of cottages set on the hillsides. In the west of the County, however, the leadmining landscape now forms a fascinating part of the County's heritage. Although the underlying geology has guided the settlement of the County, today's landscape is largely the result of human activity.

38. *Cattle grazing in the Durham Dales.*

39. *Sheep farming is widespread.*

40. *The* LIMESTONE ESCARPMENT *near Sherburn*.

41. *Meadow at* SATLEY.

Between the Wear lowlands and the North Sea lies a north-south limestone escarpment, the East Durham Plateau, which extends to the coast and is, at its highest, 700 feet above sea level. Here, in contrast to the west of the County, the limestones are magnesian, yellow rather than grey in colour, and valuable in the chemical and steel industries. This area of the County is characterised by low wooded ridges, mixed farmland and attractive cottages and villages. Growing on the escarpment itself are swathes of grassland and woodland in which survive many rare plants. East of the escarpment the land dips gently towards the cliffs which line the coast, and reveal the dramatic meeting of Durham's land and sea.

42. THE RIVER WEAR.

43. POPPYFIELDS *near Witton Gilbert.*

44. THE COAST *near Seaham*.

The County possesses 11 miles of coast where myriad streams tracing their path through the limestone cliffs to the sea have cut narrow and steep sided valleys known locally as 'denes'. The secluded and heavily wooded environment of the denes contrasts strongly with the open slopes above, and provides a home for birds and rare plants. There is peace and solitude in these lovely valleys, the best known of which is at Castle Eden, where the rare Durham Argus butterfly can be found.

45. CASTLE EDEN DENE, *near Easington*

Durham is a rural county: rivers, woods and moors provide a natural habitat
for a wide range of wildlife.

46. TAWNY OWL.

47. OTTER.

48. MALLARD HEN.

49. WATERLILY.

50. COMMON FROG.

51. DURHAM ARGUS BUTTERFLY.

52. *Man is not the only beneficiary of the County's rivers and reservoirs.*

In much of County Durham today, the landscape has retained most of the character which existed in the 18th century when agriculture dominated. Former industrial locations have been restored. The people of the County have treasured their natural inheritance and cared for it lovingly. With resourcefulness, sensitivity and careful planning they have turned the remaining legacies of industrial history into places of continuing fascination and have helped them harmonise with the environment. Careful tree planting and management has done much to restore the deciduous woodlands. Durham truly is once more a beautiful county.

53. *View towards* COWSHILL.

54. RIVERSIDE WOODS, *near Durham City*.

55. WOODLAND *in North West Durham*.

CHAPTER 3

Early History –
Settlers and Invaders

*P*eople have probably lived in the area which was to become County Durham since before the last ice age and certainly as early as 8000 - 7000 B.C, as evidence of their activities is found in the form of delicate flint and stone tools across the County.

With the mastery of metals, and the use of bronze tools from around 2000 B.C., people began clearing forests, and evidence of the development of farmsteads marked out by the first drystone walls can be seen at such places as Bracken Rigg in Teesdale. Many fine examples from this period of bronze craftsmanship, including the Gilmonby hoard and the Broomyholm shield, have been found and now grace local museums.

With the growing use of iron tools from around 700 B.C., the population spread, and there is evidence that life was not as peaceful as it had been, as farmsteads were developed inside banked and ditched enclosures. Examples are the earthworks at Cockfield Fell and cropmarks seen from the air at Elstob and West Brandon. Evidence also exists of an emerging ruling class which built hillforts, such as those still to be seen at Maiden Castle in Durham and at Redworth near Heighington. We know that the people of Durham at this time belonged to a Celtic tribe

57. *This exceptional stone, now on display at Bowes Museum, was found near Gainford and is covered with motifs usually attributed to the Late Neolithic or Early Bronze Age. County Durham is rich in these 'cup and ring' stones but little is known of their meaning or purpose.*

58. *In 1990 a hoard of Late Bronze Age metalwork was found near Gilmonby in Teesdale. The find included axes, spearheads, swords, tools and copper ingots. The hoard may have been buried by a bronzesmith for safe keeping.*

called the Brigantes - probably the largest tribe in Iron Age Britain which controlled an area stretching from the Tyne to the Humber.

Following the Roman invasion of Britain in A.D. 43, the territory of the Brigantes retained its independence until sometime between A.D. 73 and 79 when, following antagonism with the residents of this area, a series of Roman military campaigns saw the building of Dere Street, a Roman army supply route running from York to the Firth of Forth. Dere Street was guarded by earth and timber forts at Binchester (Vinovia) and Ebchester (Vindomora). At Greta Bridge (Maglona) and Bowes (Lavatrae) forts were built to guard the east - west road into Cumbria. Additional forts were built at Lanchester (Longovicium) and Chester-le-Street (Concangis) and, as Roman control was established, many were rebuilt in stone. Under Roman rule the Brigantes continued to farm in their time honoured tradition, as the Roman system of agriculture was not introduced in Durham. Britain was abandoned by the Romans around AD410 but the legacy of their occupation in County Durham can still be seen.

59. *The Roman Marching Camp near* REY CROSS *is bisected by the modern A66 which is on the line of the Roman road.*

60. *This* ROMAN ALTAR, *now on display at the Josephine and John Bowes Museum, was originally erected in a small shrine on the moor at Scargill near Barningham in Teesdale.*

61. *The remains of the hypocaust, part of the underfloor central heating system at the* ROMAN FORT OF VINOVIA *at Binchester near Bishop Auckland.*

The next wave of invaders, the Angles and the Saxons, came from the northern coast of Germany and Denmark and these earliest English people are mainly known from their rich pagan burial sites found in the east of Durham, close to Easington and Castle Eden. Other evidence they left behind includes place names such as Seaham, Easington and Seaton. By AD600 the English had taken control of the whole area which was to become the County, accepted Christianity, and established two separate kingdoms - Bernicia, which extended from north of the Tees, and Deira to the south - which together formed Anglo-Saxon Northumbria. For two centuries the kingdom grew and prospered, towns developed and the glory of the Northumbrian Church rose in importance. By AD 800 the kingdom was in decline and, weakened by border wars and

62. 7TH CENTURY ANGLO SAXON GOLD PENDANT *found at Sacriston.*

63. 9TH/10TH CENTURY CARVED BONE STRIP *Anglo Saxon Scandinavian style, found at Ferryhill.*

internal feuding, was open to further invasion.

Viking invaders from Denmark and Norway first raided the North East coast at Lindisfarne in A.D. 793. On this occasion they merely looted and withdrew. The Norsemen were, however, also skilled traders, craftsmen, and farmers, and by the 9th century, through trade and more organised military conquest, they had come to control large areas of eastern England. By the end of the 9th century, the Viking kingdom of York controlled northern England, with Durham and the rest of Northumbria very much within its influence.

In the west of County Durham, in the upper reaches of the Pennine Dales, Norse-Irish settlers from Norwegian viking colonies in Ireland moved into the area, creating villages and farms such as Ireshopeburn, in Weardale, and Simy Folds, in Teesdale. At Simy Folds, the deserted and evocative remains of a Viking farm can still be seen sheltering beneath the high moors.

Norse domination lasted until A.D. 954 when the last Viking king of York, Eric Bloodaxe, was ambushed and slain as he crossed Stainmore in Teesdale. Today, the lonely sight of ancient Rey Cross, next to the A66, stands to provide a reminder of the passing of this last Viking, and ancient border conflict.

It was during the late 10th and early 11th centuries that England was to become a unified country and Durham as a county was to take

64. HOLWICK 'GREEN TROD' - *the ancient drovers' route from Scotland to Yorkshire over Cronkley Fell.*

65. The long narrow strips of land running back from houses in Mickleton Village have the same boundaries as in the Middle Ages.

shape. The Community of St. Cuthbert found a home and resting place for Cuthbert's remains at Durham in A.D. 995. The community had by this time become immensely influential in secular as well religious matters. It had been granted large estates of land between the Rivers Tyne and Tees by, amongst others, Cnut (Canute), the King of Denmark, and also of Norway, and, by the early 11th century, of England too, who made a pilgrimage to Durham at that time.

The influence and wealth of the church had become well established. Later it was the powerful and ruthless William the Conqueror who granted the Bishops of Durham princely powers, thus creating the palatine of County Durham.

66. ROUTEMARKER, *near Stanhope.*

67. THE KEEP, DURHAM CASTLE - *The Castle was founded by William the Conqueror in 1072 as a stronghold for controlling the area and was totally rebuilt in 1839-40.*

The Norman Conquest of England in 1066 was not initially accepted in the north. The absorption of Durham into the Norman Kingdom was a difficult and bloody process and continued up to 1080. The Domesday Book has no entry for Durham or Northumberland. This has been interpreted as an acknowledgement by William I that he had an incomplete hold on the area and did not at that stage consider it fully part of his Kingdom. The Normans built a motte-and-bailey castle at Durham around 1071-2, but it was an isolated stronghold and beyond its walls the countryside was not secure. Gradually, however, control was established and lands in County Durham were given to those Normans who had accompanied William in his original invasion at Hastings. For example, Guy de Baliol was granted land in Teesdale and his nephew, Bernard, built the castle at Barnard

Castle on an imposing cliff overlooking the Tees in around 1093. At Bowes is another Norman keep, built on the site of the former Roman Fort. The foundation stone for Durham Cathedral was laid in 1093 adjacent to the site of the White Church formerly built as a shrine to St Cuthbert. Within 40 years the main phase of the magnificent Norman cathedral had been completed. It is likely that by the end of the 11th century the people of this area had accepted the Normans as the new rulers. The granting of powers of a military and secular nature to the Bishop of Durham effectively created an enclave where the Bishop had all the powers normally exercised by the King.

68. BOWES KEEP, TEESDALE *A Norman castle built on the site of the former Roman Fort.*

69. THE GATEHOUSE, DURHAM CASTLE *was founded in the late 12th century.*

70. BARNARD CASTLE *built by Bernard Baliol on the banks of the River Tees in 1093.*

71. *Engraving of* BARNARD CASTLE.

72. DURHAM CATHEDRAL *from the River Wear*.

73 FRAMWELLGATE BRIDGE *was built originally around 1128.*
A gatehouse stood at the east side and a chapel in the middle. The present structure was built after 1401.

CHAPTER 4

Durham's Place in Christian History

*T*he late architectural historian, Sir Nikolaus Pevsner, wrote "Durham is one of the great experiences of Europe to the eyes of those who appreciate architecture...The group of cathedral, castle, and monastery on the rock can be compared only to Avignon and Prague...". Some would say Durham, a World Heritage Site, is superior to either, and one of the world's greatest statements of Christian faith.

Although the Roman Empire accepted Christianity in the early 4th century AD, there is little evidence of Christianity in this area until the 7th century. It was King Oswald, a Saxon, who brought Aidan (St. Aidan) from Iona to found the monastery on Lindisfarne (Holy Island) just off the Northumbrian coast. Monasteries were also founded at Hartlepool in 647, at Wearmouth in 674 and at Jarrow in 681.

Cuthbert, hermit, Prior, Bishop and one of the founding fathers of the Northumbrian Church, died in A.D. 687. Famous during his life, he became even more so after his death and churches throughout the north were named after him. He was buried in St. Peter's Church, Lindisfarne, and when exhumed in 698 it was recorded that his body was miraculously incorrupt.

Monks working in the scriptorium, or writing room, at Lindisfarne produced the Lindisfarne Gospels and the Durham Gospels. The Lindisfarne Gospels, produced in about 698 in honour of St. Cuthbert, are in the British Library. The Durham Gospels are at Durham Cathedral.

After the first Viking raid on Lindisfarne in 793, the Community of St. Cuthbert abandoned Lindisfarne, taking with it the Saint's relics. A journey, long in both distance and time, ensued, first to Norham-on-Tweed and ending at Chester-le-Street in 883, where the Community built a wooden church on the present site of the Church of St. Mary and St. Cuthbert. There the venerable Community settled for over 100 years during which it acquired secular powers and

much wealth. Further Viking raids caused the Community to move again and legend has it that during its travels it was told in a vision to

75. *The* PECTORAL CROSS OF ST CUTHBERT, *may be seen in the Treasury at Durham Cathedral.*

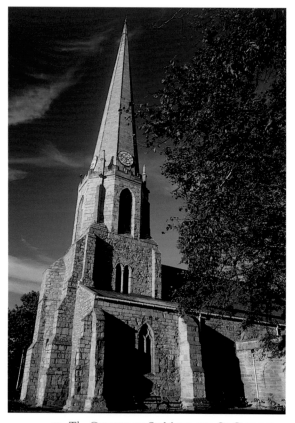

76. *The* CHURCH OF ST MARY AND ST CUTHBERT, *Chester-le-Street, dates from the late Anglo-Saxon period and was rebuilt in the 18th century and was restored in 1862.*

77. BISHOP DE PUISET'S BIBLE, *may be seen in the Treasury at Durham Cathedral.*

78. ST CUTHBERT'S SHRINE, *Durham Cathedral*.

take St. Cuthbert's remains to Dunholm, the hill island - the magnificent rocky peninsula formed by the River Wear and the heart of today's City of Durham. Here, in 995, Bishop Ealdhun, the first Bishop of Durham, built a stone cathedral with twin towered bronze pinnacles, which became known as the White Church, as a shrine to St. Cuthbert.

Reference has already been made to the difficulty experienced by the Normans in subduing the people of this area, and Durham was recognised as a strategic and readily defensible site. In addition to the building of the castle, powers were granted to the Bishop of Durham to raise his own army, administer civil and criminal law, mint his own coins, create Barons of the Bishopric, levy taxes, negotiate and make truces, grant charters and claim rights. The position of Bishop of Durham became, in effect, the second most powerful office in the country. A Benedictine monastery was established in 1083 and the foundations of Durham Cathedral were laid by the Norman Bishop, William de St. Calais in 1093. The use of transverse and rib vaulting on massive decorated columns in its construction was an architectural innovation of great importance. The main body of the Cathedral was completed in only 40 years, an amazing piece of engineering and marvellously symbolic of the power of the Church.

79. Durham Cathedral *and the* Fulling Mill, *Durham City*.

80. *Engraving of* DURHAM CATHEDRAL.

81. THE DLI CHAPEL in *Durham Cathedral,*
flanked by the famous Norman Pillars.

82. DURHAM CATHEDRAL.

83. MILLENNIUM WINDOW, *Durham Cathedral.*

84. *The* HIGH ALTAR *and* ROSE WINDOW, *Durham Cathedral.*

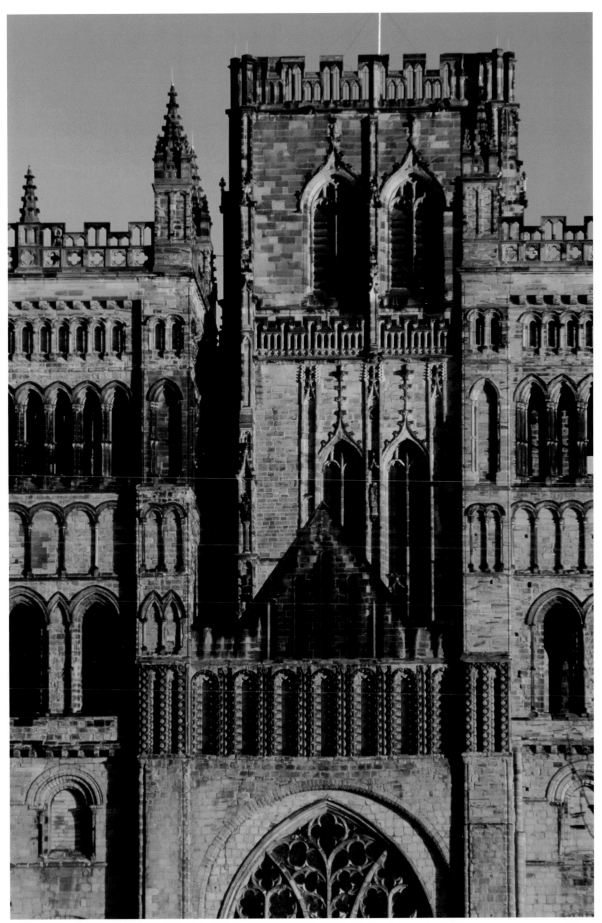

85. *Sunset*, DURHAM CATHEDRAL.

86. Durham Cathedral *from Wharton Park.*

87. Durham Cathedral *from Durham Railway Station.*

88. Durham Cathedral *from the south east.*

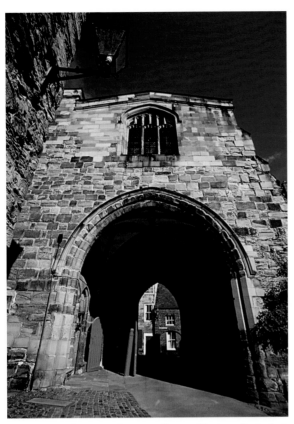

89. GATE TO COLLEGE GREEN, *Durham Cathedral*.

90. PREBENDS BRIDGE *in Durham City was built in 1772-5 at the expense of the Canons or Prebends of Durham Cathedral.*

91. *The Gothic style 'CONDUIT HOUSE' on College Green, Durham City, was built in 1751 as a water tower.*

92. THE CHURCH OF ST JOHN THE EVANGELIST *at Escomb.*

The spread of Christianity led to the building of other churches throughout County Durham. Two of the earliest were built of stone and still survive. The most complete seventh century church is that of St. John the Evangelist at Escomb which was probably built between 670 and 690. The stone used in its construction was taken from the Roman fort at nearby Binchester. Fragments of glass discovered during recent excavations were found to be identical with glass from the sites of Wearmouth and Jarrow monasteries. St Mary's Church at Seaham is a foundation of late seventh or early eighth century and the worked stone used in its construction is thought to have come from a Roman signal station which may have stood nearby. Pre-Conquest stone crosses and sculptures may be seen across the County with particularly fine examples at St. Andrew's Auckland at South Church, at St. Mary's in Gainford and at Durham Cathedral.

93. THE CHURCH OF ST MARY THE VIRGIN *at Seaham is of 7th/8th century origin.*

94 and 95. LATE 10TH CENTURY CARVED STONE CROSS SHAFTS *showing Viking influence*.

96. ST EDMUND'S PARISH CHURCH, *Sedgefield, is a 12th century building on the
site of the original wooden Saxon building built around 900 A.D.*

97. THE CHURCH OF ST MARGARET OF ANTIOCH, *in Durham has been much altered but is of 12th century foundation. It features the original Norman windows, and a Frosterley marble font.*

98. EGGLESTONE ABBEY, *Barnard Castle.*

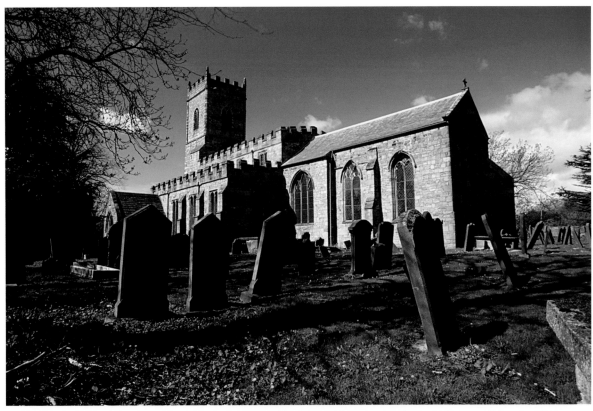

99. LANCHESTER ALL SAINTS' CHURCH *was built c1147, extended in the 13th century and contains five monolithic pillars from the Roman Fort at Longevicium.*

100. ST GILES' CHURCH AT BOWES - *mainly late mediaeval in origin although heavily restored in the 19th century. Much of the stone came from the nearby Roman Fort.*

Wearmouth and Jarrow monasteries became centres of knowledge; both had extensive libraries and scriptoria producing beautifully illuminated manuscripts. Jarrow was the home of the Venerable Bede (673 - 735), the father of English history. We owe much of our knowledge of Northumbria to his Ecclesiastical History of the English Church and People written in 731. The remains of St. Bede, also known as the Venerable Bede, were removed to Durham Cathedral from Jarrow in 1092. This further enhanced the importance of the Cathedral as a place of pilgrimage.

Durham Cathedral continues to play a vital role in the life of the County and the Region, as it has done for 1,000 years. It remains at the heart of the Diocese of Durham and welcomes over 500,000 visitors each year from all over the world.

101. *Engraving of Finchale Abbey.*

102. ST. BEDE'S TOMB *in the* GALILEE CHAPEL, *Durham Cathedral.*

103. FINCHALE ABBEY ON THE RIVER WEAR *near Durham, once served as a retreat for monks from the Abbey at Durham and was built in the 13th century on the site formerly settled by the hermit St Godric.*

CHAPTER 5

The Middle Ages –
The Age of the Prince Bishops

As a frontier county, Durham continued to require special treatment from the King. He granted secular powers for the Bishops of Durham in addition to their ecclesiastical powers. Durham Castle was strengthened with the enclosure of virtually the whole of the peninsula and became the Bishop's Palace, administrative centre and fortified stronghold.

William de St. Calais was the first 'Prince Bishop' and his powers resembled more closely those of the Prince Bishops of Germany than those of senior English clerics. He benefited from privileges such as freedom from the obligation to provide military support for the King. The Scots however posed a continuing threat to peace and there were invasions in 1136, 1138 and 1141.

In 1183 Hugh de Puiset made a survey of his lands to assess the tax payable to him as a temporal Lord. The results were compiled as the Boldon Book and this survey tells us that most of the County's distinctive open village greens date from this period, that farming was mostly pastoral, and that most of the population was under obligation to the Bishop, being required to carry out a range of tasks, including fencing, carrying, helping with hunts and mining. Mineral exploitation occurred in the west where de

Puiset had royal permission to mine silver and lead in Weardale. Iron ore was also extracted and was smelted and forged with charcoal. A single coal mine was being worked at Escomb. The See of Durham reached its peak under de Puiset in 1189 and Durham became a County Palatine - set apart from the rest of the country by the fact that the Bishop could exercise powers which elsewhere only the King could exercise.

The power and wealth of the mediaeval church can be seen from surviving buildings. The Benedictine Order built an abbey on a lovely wooded bend on the River Wear, at Finchale near Durham, after 1196. Egglestone Abbey, south east of Barnard Castle, was founded in 1195 for the White (Premonstratensian) Canons. By the 13th century most of Durham's collegiate churches had been created and staffed

by a college of canons with a dean at their head. They were richly endowed with land and property. These include St. Andrew Auckland at South Church, one of the largest parishes in the County, All Saints' at Lanchester, St. Mary and St. Cuthbert at Chester-le-Street and St. Mary at Staindrop.

The Prince Bishops also founded several hospitals and almshouses. Kepier Hospital, just outside the ancient city of Durham, was founded in 1112 by Bishop Flambard. Today, only the 14th century gatehouse survives. Nearby are the remains of the Hospital of St. Mary Magdalene, founded in the mid twelfth century. Much larger in scale was Sherburn Hospital, founded in 1181 as a leper hospital, which although largely rebuilt, has parts of the original chapel and gatehouse.

105. THE CHAPEL OF ST MARY MAGDALENE, *Durham City*.

106. The church of St. Mary the Virgin, *Staindrop, has Saxon and 12th, 13th, and 14th century features.*

107. St Oswald's Church, *Durham, was founded between the 12th and 14th centuries.*

108. EGGLESTONE ABBEY, *on a mid winter evening.*

109. THE CLOISTERS, *Durham Cathedral.*

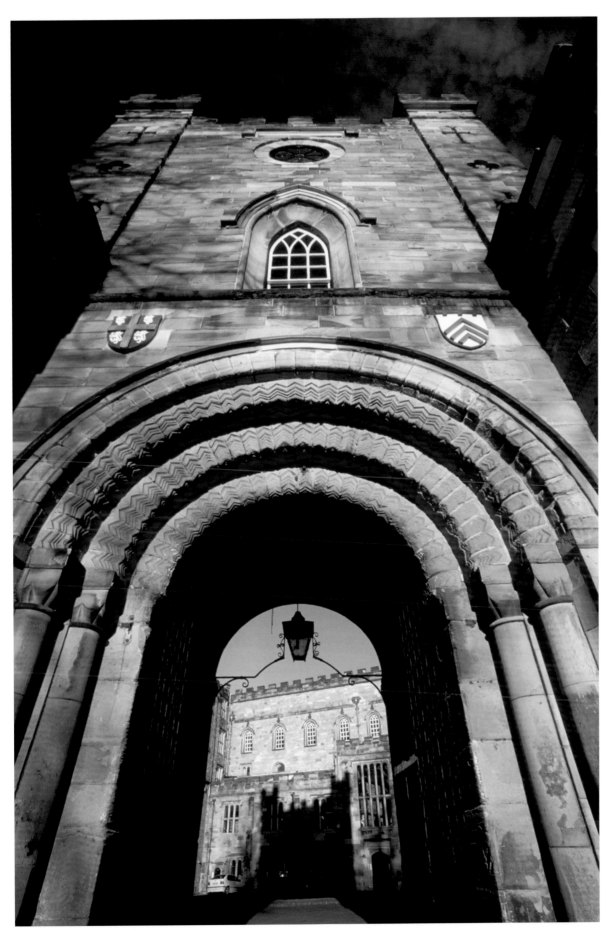

110. GATEWAY TO DURHAM CASTLE.

The Bishops had other residences besides Durham Castle. The Bishop's Palace at Bishop Auckland was begun by Hugh de Puiset as a manor and hunting lodge around 1183 and was much altered during the 17th and 18th centuries. Traces of another hunting lodge remain at Westgate in Weardale and the Bishops' deer park lay between Eastgate and Westgate. At Easington, near the coast, is Seaton Holme, a large 13th century house used as a retirement home by Bishop Nicholas Farnham in 1249.

The Prior of Durham Monastery was the Bishop of Durham's powerful ecclesiastical neighbour on the peninsula and had considerable revenues from about twenty manors which had been given to the Monastery by successive Bishops.

The remains of two of these manor houses survive at Muggleswick in north west Durham and Bearpark (Beaurepaire) near Durham City which was built in 1258 and largely destroyed by the Scots in 1640-44. Earthworks remain of the Prior's manor near Pittington and one of his tithe barns stands fully intact in Hallgarth Street, in Durham City.

The power of the lords temporal, the aristocratic families, is shown in the string of great castles running from north east to south west across the County. These are to be found at Lumley, Brancepeth, Witton, Raby, and Barnard Castle. Raby Castle, set in beautiful parkland, is built partly of stone from Barnard Castle. Raby was a stronghold for the Nevilles, the County's most noteworthy family in mediaeval times. Ralph

111. Engraving of the Bishop's retreat, at Beaurepaire (now Bearpark).

112. Raby Castle

113. Raby Castle gardens

114. *A string of great castles runs through County Durham.*
Here the 11th century Lumley Castle *can be seen in its rural setting.*

115. LUMLEY CASTLE.

Neville, whose tomb is to be found in Staindrop Church, defeated the Scots at the Battle of Neville's Cross in 1346. The invasion of northern England by the Scots, who were allied with the French, was partly a diversionary tactic to slow English military success in France following the Battle of Crécy, and partly a result of continuing tensions between England and Scotland. The defeat of the 12,000-strong Scottish army by an English army of possibly only 5,000 led to the capture of the Scottish King. The Neville family later became Earls of Westmorland and were deeply involved in Plantagenet politics during the Wars of the Roses. Cecily, a daughter of the house, and famous as the 'Rose of Raby', was the mother of Edward IV and Richard III.

Splendid Brancepeth Castle was also a Neville seat, and Witton Castle was probably built as a manor house around 1370, and fortified in 1410, by the Eure family. Magnificent Lumley Castle, now an hotel, is beautifully preserved. A licence to crenellate was granted to Sir Ralph Lumley in 1392 by the Bishop of Durham and the castle remains essentially as it was built.

As everywhere on the Scottish border in the mediaeval period, lesser landowners in the County built tower houses and bastles for safety, and several survive, often disguised as later buildings. Most date from the 13th to 15th centuries and include Witton Tower at Witton-le-Wear, Langleydale Old Lodge on the Raby Estate, Dalden Tower at Dalton-le-Dale, near Seaham, and Baal Hill House, near Wolsingham.

116. *The remains of* DALDEN TOWER *in Dalton-le-Dale, A fortification dating from the time of Edward II.*

117. *The remains of the 15th century* PELE TOWER *at Ludworth.*

118. BRANCEPETH CASTLE.

119. ELVET BRIDGE, *Durham City*.

In the early middle ages County Durham was sparsely populated. Durham, a borough by 1180, was the only town of any size. Barnard Castle, a borough before 1167 had become an established centre of population in the west. Most settlements were developed, or redeveloped, after the Norman Conquest during the 12th and 13th centuries around a green. As well as providing a focus for local events, the central green could be used for common grazing or even defensively if the entrance to the village was barricaded. Villages were of two main types: 'two row', where the cottages and houses extended along both sides of the main street and green, or 'four row' where they enclosed the green on all four sides. Examples of the former are Shincliffe and Shadforth, and of the latter Sedgefield and Easington. Other villages were established at crossroads.

While some early settlements in the County grew and prospered, others declined or disappeared. These are referred to as shrunken or deserted villages. The reasons for the declines are various and probably include crop failures, agricultural change, and plague. Often the only record of these villages in the landscape is the telltale contours of former houses, roads and field boundaries now buried underground, or the characteristic ridged marks of mediaeval ploughing.

The beginning of the County's great industries is traceable to the 13th and 14th centuries. A 13th century iron smelting site survives at Bedburn and the exploitation of lead and silver from the Dales generated huge wealth for the Bishops of Durham. Collapsed bell-pits for the extraction of coal can be seen at Cockfield Fell. During the relatively peaceful 15th century, agriculture continued to progress without interruption and a study of the records for the Prior's Manor at Elvet Hall show that revenues from corn continued to rise.

120. Shincliffe Village.

121. Sedgefield Village.

122. Bowlees Village.

CHAPTER 6

The Sixteenth to Eighteenth Centuries

*A*fter a peaceful 15th century the 16th was quite the reverse. In 1536 Henry VIII saw the independence of the 'Prince Bishops' as a potential threat to the authority of the monarchy and removed much of their power. That year the 'Pilgrimage of Grace' occurred as a movement embracing the whole of the north in which most of the Durham nobility took part - including the Nevilles and the Lumleys whose aims were the restoration of the Roman Catholic religion and the restoration of the Palatinate powers to the Bishop. The 'Pilgrimage' was ruthlessly overcome in 1537 and Roger Lumley was executed.

The year 1541 saw the dissolution of the Monastery at Durham. The last Prior became the first Dean and the monks became the first prebendaries, taking over the ownership of the Monastery lands. Finchale and Egglestone Priories were abandoned and the shrines of St. Cuthbert and the Venerable Bede in the Cathedral were vandalised - although when the body of St. Cuthbert was found to be still incorrupt, no further damage was done.

The Rising of the Northern Earls in 1569 was an ill-judged and ill-fated revolt in support of Mary Queen of Scots in which war again came to the County. Brancepeth Castle and Raby Castle were forfeit to the Crown due to the Nevilles' support for Mary. The late sixteenth and early seventeenth centuries saw the decline of other landed families, and the rise of more entrepreneurial successors whose wealth was derived from the exploitation of coal.

The accession of James VI of Scotland as James I of England in 1603, brought, in theory, an end to the cross-border conflicts of earlier centuries, and the need to fortify buildings against attack. A new style of architecture developed and two excellent examples of this type of non-fortified domestic building survive. The first is Horden Hall, a small manor house built for Sir John Conyers in the first half of the 17th century. The second is Gainford Hall built by the Reverend John Craddock in about 1603. The best example of a town house containing building work of the 17th century is Blagrave's House in Barnard Castle. West Auckland Old Hall at West Green also dates from this period. Unthank Hall across the Wear from Stanhope and Whitfield Cottages in Wolsingham are further examples. Several 17th century farmhouses survive such as Levy Pool near Bowes, Cragside, and Westerhopeburn in Weardale.

124. GAINFORD HALL *dates from c1600 and was heavily restored during the 19th century.*

125. BLAGRAVE'S HOUSE, *Barnard Castle, dates from the 17th century and contains a vaulted cellar which may be mediaeval.*

With the Restoration, the powers of the Bishop and Dean were restored and Bishop John Cosin, the first Bishop after 1660, restored and enlarged his palace at Bishop Auckland, decorated many churches, and endowed almshouses at Durham.

After the Jacobite Rebellion of 1715 more of the old landowning class was dispossessed in favour of individuals from trade and industry, particularly coal-mining. Several families whose fortunes had been made in the coal trade, including the Liddells of Ravensworth, purchased estates in the County. They made their mark by building new houses or altering old ones in the elegant palladian or classical style, spending their wealth with taste. At about the same time, Sir John Vanbrugh altered Lumley Castle and in 1760 Croxdale Hall was rebuilt for the Salvins.

126. THE ALMSHOUSES *in Durham City were re-built by Bishop Cosin in 1668 and also included a grammar and a song schools.*

127. BEAMISH HALL NEAR STANLEY *dates from before 1620 and has been remodelled and extended several times.*

128. HORSLEY HALL *near Eastgate in Weardale dates from the 17th Century.*

129. HAMSTERLEY HALL *was built around 1770 but includes remains of earlier structures*.

130. CASTLE EDEN HALL *dates from 1758*.

131. STANHOPE OLD HALL *is mediaeval in origin and was extensively remodelled during the 16th and 17th centuries.*

132. GATEWAY TO THE BISHOP'S PALACE *at Bishop Auckland.*

Like Elemore Hall, near Pittington, rebuilt in 1749-53 for George Baker, Croxdale Hall and others contain fine plasterwork by Italian craftsmen. Beamish Hall, rebuilt in 1737 for William Davidson, was passed to the Shafto family. Castle Eden Hall with its Gothic embellishments was designed for the Burdon family in the 1790s. Also in the gothic style is Hamsterley Hall near Ebchester rebuilt in about 1770. Probably the finest Palladian House in the County is Rokeby Park in Teesdale, built between 1725 and 1730. Examples of modest late 18th century houses are Shotton Hall and Bowes Hall. Many of these fine homes were surrounded by elegant landscaped parkland as can still be seen at Hardwick Hall near Sedgefield and at Castle Eden Hall. With their range of features including lakes, grottos, and banqueting houses, these sites are both acknowledged as being of national importance.

Elsewhere the landscape was being transformed by enclosure, which had begun in the mid-16th century with the end of the strip field system of cultivation and the conversion of more land to pasture land for rearing livestock. Around 75,000 acres, 12% of the total land area of the County, but almost all in the low lying east, had been enclosed by 1750. After 1750 more land was enclosed in Weardale and Teesdale. Much was higher ground on the fells and moors and may be distinguished today by the picturesque drystone walls. Many of the enclosures involved Acts of Parliament and involved huge areas. Lanchester Common included 15,000 acres and Wolsingham Common 10,000. The County became self-sufficient in meat and dairy products and supplied neighbouring Tyneside, Wearside and Teesside. Improved husbandry and stock breeding was practised, producing for example, the famous Durham shorthorn cow.

133. MORTHAM TOWER, *near Brignall Mill, was built in the 14th century as a tower house. Thomas Rokeby added more spacious living quarters in the late 15th century.*

134. CHESTER NEW BRIDGE, *near Chester-le-Street, is mediaeval in origin and carries the south west drive from Lambton Castle across the Wear.*

135. THE DEER HOUSE AT AUCKLAND CASTLE
built by Bishop Trevor in 1760.

136. THE BUTTER MARKET, *Barnard Castle, built in 1747.*
The upper floor was made into a Courtroom in 1814.

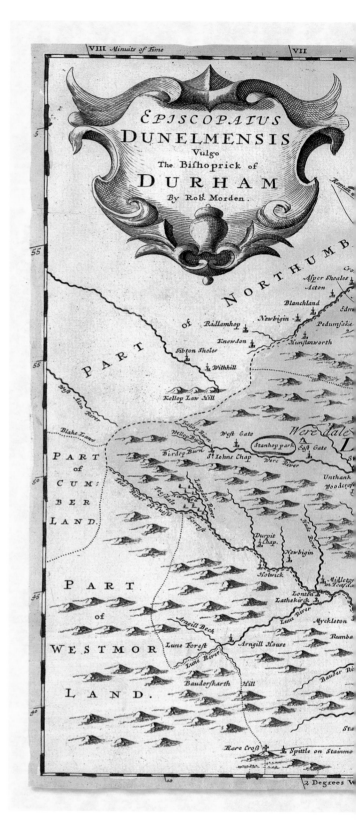

At the start of the 19th century Durham remained essentially a rural county with a population of 149,354 The largest town was Durham City with a population of 7,636. Barnard Castle and Bishop Auckland had

populations of over 2,000. Only four others, Wolsingham, Chester-le-Street, Sedgefield and Staindrop had populations of over 1,000. Increasing trade and industry had led to the growth in numbers of the merchant class and of professional people in the larger towns, particularly Durham. In the 18th century they built fine town houses, many of which still exist in Saddler Street and the North and South Baileys.

137. OLD DURHAM GARDENS, *near Durham City - an area settled as early as the Iron Age.*
The Gazebo was founded in the 17th century.

138. WESTERHOPE BURN FARM, *near Eastgate.*

139. COTTAGES *at Raby Castle date from the 18th century.*

140. DOORWAY, *Durham City.*

141. DOORWAY, *Durham City.*

CHAPTER 7

Industrial Expansion

*A*longside the developments in agriculture, the 18th century saw the early appearance of heavy industries. County Durham had an almost unrivalled advantage of economic location which incorporated enormous reserves of the finest quality coking coal in the Durham Coalfield, deposits of iron ore in west Durham (and the nearby great reserves of the Cleveland Hills) and rivers for building ships and loading and unloading their cargoes. The nineteenth century saw the transformation of the County to one of the most industrialised in the country and the development of the great peppering of small settlements which today give this County its unique character.

Coal had been mined since mediaeval times and by 1527 was being exported to London through Newcastle, having been won chiefly in the Bishop's mines in the 'Grand Lease' of the Manors of Gateshead and Whickham. Early extraction was by bell pits or drifts such as in the Chester-le-Street and Lanchester areas and near Raby. Newcastle's monopoly on the export of coal was broken during the Civil War when the Wear was developed as a rival shipping river. Access to deeper coal became possible in the early 18th century through the use of pumps powered by steam engines and as coal reserves near rivers were exhausted and new

seams exploited elsewhere, railed wagonways were developed to transport coal to rivers for export.

Horses were used to pull wagons along wagon ways which were initially made wholly of wood and later benefited from rails of iron or steel. With improvements, by the mid 18th century wagonways could be up to eight miles long. In 1805 the motive power of the horse began to be replaced by stationary steam engines hauling strings of wagons by rope and cable. An outstanding monument to the wagonway is the stone arch over the Causey Burn near Tanfield which was designed and built in 1725-26 by a local stone mason, Ralph Wood. Causey Arch, the world's first railway bridge, carried coal from collieries in the Tanfield area to the Tyne. Standing 80 feet high and over 100 feet long, at the time it was the longest single span bridge in the world.

143. CAUSEY ARCH *at Tanfield is the world's first railway bridge and was built in 1725-26.*

144. *An early engraving of Seaham Harbour.*

Control of the output from Durham collieries began as early as the 17th century and was further formalised with the 'Regulation of the Vend' in 1708. In 1726 the Grand Allies cartel was created between some of the major coal owners who successfully regulated the market, controlling not only production but also transport of coal over wagonways to ships for export.

Coal output dramatically increased with the development of the East Durham coalfield from the 1820s. Here the high quality coal seams were overlaid by magnesian limestone and winning a colliery was initially an expensive business. Most of the villages which developed around these collieries were entirely new rather than based on an existing settlement. A witness to a Royal Commission in 1841 noted that "Within the last ten or twelve years an entirely new population has been produced. Where

formerly there was not the single hut of a shepherd, the lofty steam engine chimneys of a colliery now send their columns of smoke into the sky and in the vicinity a town is called, as if by enchantment, into immediate existence".

One of the towns created in this period was unusual - Seaham Harbour. Lord Londonderry, one of the most prominent landowners in the area, shipped coal from his collieries through the port of Sunderland where he paid dues. In 1828 he began to create his own port at Seaham, which was a small sleepy fishing hamlet with an open beach where Lord Byron had courted Anne Isabella Milbanke. Lord Londonderry also planned a town, designed by Newcastle architect John Dobson. The first coals were shipped from the North Dock in 1831, and although the town did not develop as planned, some traces of the original intentions can be seen today.

145. By 1929 dock exports of coal at SEAHAM HARBOUR reached an all time high of 2,300,000 tons annually and remained high until the 1950s.

146. The Londonderrys' plans to create a harbour at SEAHAM were a great success but plans for a magnificent town with a central crescent foundered due to lack of money.

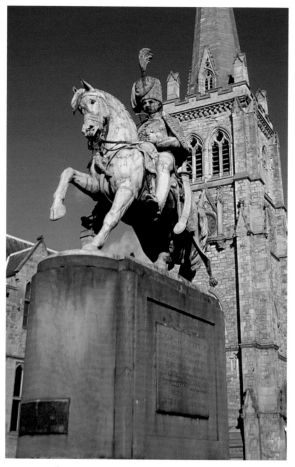

147. STATUE OF THE 3RD MARQUIS OF LONDONDERRY, Market Place, Durham City.

The Durham coalfield was extensive and by 1901 well over 100,000 people were employed in the extraction of coal. Many of the settlements were new and Methodism became a popular form of religion in the new mining communities, preferred for its simplicity, fervour and absence of ritual. Coal miners supported institutions they created themselves, such as co-operative stores, welfare institutes and above all trade unions. The Durham Miners' Association was formed in 1869 and three years later achieved the abolition of the 'miners' bond', whereby miners were required to bind themselves to an employer for a year. The Association was led by such great men as Peter Lee, after whom one of the County's new towns created since the last world war was named. In 1871 the first of many Miners' Galas (the Big Meeting) was held in which miners from the many collieries marched into Durham behind their colliery banners. By 1911 nearly 152,000 miners were employed, almost 30% of the County's workforce, and 1913 saw maximum coal output when the Northern Coalfield, of which 70% was the Durham Coalfield, produced 58.7 million tons, almost one quarter of the then national total. Coal mining became a nationalised industry on 1st January 1947 when there were 127 collieries in the County producing a saleable output of 24,530,000 tons annually.

148. *The former* DEAN AND CHAPTER COLLIERY, *Ferryhill*.

149. COLLIERY BANNERS *at the Durham Big Meeting, the first of which was held in 1871.*

150 THE MINERS' HALL *in Durham City, built in 1913-15 for the Durham Miners' Association,
replaced the former Hall in North Road.*

Although Durham produced good quality coal, conditions underground were often appalling. The seams were often shallow and wet and explosive gas a frequent problem. Many miners were injured or killed in underground accidents. In a three year period from 1876-78 there were 116 deaths in the Durham coalfield from roof falls. A number of major accidents caused great loss of life and devastated whole mining communities and the causes of these were various. At Seaham Colliery on 8th September 1880, 168 men and boys died in an explosion caused by underground shot blasting. On 29th May 1951 at Easington, the pick blade of a coal cutter struck a rock causing a spark which ignited an explosion, killing 81 miners. Two rescue workers also died. County Durham has not forgotten the sacrifice of those miners who gave their lives and memorials can be found in many locations. The achievement of the Durham miners is also commemorated in a splendid stained glass window in County Hall, Durham.

151. MINERS' MEMORIAL WINDOW
at County Hall, Durham.

During the mid 19th century in the North Pennines lead mining was peaking. Like coal mining it was of mediaeval or even earlier origin but was reorganised during the 18th century by large companies. The first of these, the London Lead Company, was formed in 1692 and established its northern headquarters at Middleton-in-Teesdale. The W.B. Lead Company had its Durham headquarters in Ireshopeburn and worked mainly in Weardale.

152. THE BAINBRIDGE MEMORIAL FOUNTAIN,
in Middleton-in-Teesdale.

153. FORMER LEADMINING BUILDINGS, *at Hudeshope, near Middleton-in-Teesdale.*

154. THE CHIMNEY AT SIKEHEAD LEAD MINE *near Hunstanworth in Weardale.*

Lead ore was extracted by making an adit (a near horizontal tunnel) until the vein was reached or by 'hushing' in which veins of ore were exposed by releasing dammed water-courses which washed away the topsoil, the effects of which can still be seen as interesting features in the landscape. The lead ore was crushed and separated from waste originally by hand, but from the mid-nineteenth century by machinery, such as can still be seen at the Killhope Lead Mining Centre where the W.B. Lead Company installed, in 1874, a great iron water wheel 34 feet in diameter.

155. *A landscape showing the scars of leadmining including the 'COLDBERRY GUTTER',
a leadmining hush breaking the skyline at Hudeshope near Middleton-in-Teesdale.*

156. Killhope Lead Mining Centre.

157. *Underground at* Killhope Lead Mining Centre.

Smelt mills, where the ore was heated and processed to extract the lead, were established at places such as Rookhope, Stanhope, Bollihope and Egglestone. Many lead miners were also farmers on a small scale as the food they produced was needed to supplement their meagre income from mining. The lead mining companies were paternalistic, building houses, schools, mechanics' institutes and reading rooms. While coal exports from the Tyne and Wear doubled between the 1730s and 1800, lead production in Weardale rose more than sixfold and while coal was mainly shipped to London, lead entered world-wide trade. The lead mines of the Dales played a key role in enabling Britain to be the world's largest single producer of lead and were an important element in the country's economy at that time. The story of the miners who made this possible and of their families is told at the Killhope Lead Mining Centre today.

158. ROOKHOPE ARCH - *one of a series of arches which once carried the flues of the Lintzgarth Lead Smelter.*

159. HEDLEY HILL COKE OVENS, *near Hedley Hope.*

160. SWORD MILL, *Shotley Bridge.*
Swordmakers arrived from Solingen in Germany in the late 17th century bringing world famous craftsmen to the area.

161. *Aerial view of the former* CONSETT STEELWORKS. *This site has now been completely reclaimed.*

The remains of beehive ovens used in early manufacture of coke are scattered across the County in places such as East Hedley Hope, and near Tow Law. The country's first production of coke by-products, including sulphate of ammonia, benzol oil and coal tar took place at Crook. At Derwentcote, near Ebchester, are the substantial remains of an early 18th century steel cementation furnace, the only one of its kind surviving. Other iron and steelworks grew including those of the Weardale Iron Company at Tow Law which from 1845 turned a single farm into a town with a population of 2,000. It was a similar story at Witton Park and also at Spennymoor where the earliest steel produced was used to make the rails laid across the High Level Bridge at Newcastle. By 1860 the County had 58 ironworks with blast furnaces. From 1840 the Derwent Iron Company transformed the

hamlet of Conside with a population of 195 into the town of Consett with a population of 4,953 by 1841. By 1875 the works were owned by the Consett Iron Company which employed up to 6,000 men and was by a long way the country's largest producer of iron ship plates which were used on the Rivers Tyne and Wear.

162. DERWENTCOTE STEEL FURNACE *was built in 1733 and remained in use until about 1875. It is one of only two preserved examples in the country.*

163. *The former* CONSETT STEELWORKS.

Shipbuilding on the Tyne and Wear developed rapidly after 1850, with record tonnages of naval and merchant ships being produced. Steam, and later turbine, driven steel ships dramatically changed the world and its economy. By the turn of the twentieth century, over a quarter of the world's new ships were being built in north east yards creating enormous demand for local steel and coal.

Hand in hand with the development of all these industrial activities was the invention of a new means of transport for raw materials which was also dramatically to transform the world. This was the development of colliery wagonways into railways. The steam railway locomotive was developed by George Stephenson and with funds supplied by local businessman, Edward Pease, the first passenger railway in the world, the Stockton and Darlington Railway, was opened in 1825 with his locomotive, 'Locomotion', pulling 80 tons of coal together with passengers at 10-12 miles per hour. The railway extended to Shildon and from Shildon to Witton Park, a section over which it was rope hauled. At Shildon the world's first railway station was built and, nearby, Timothy Hackworth founded his Soho Locomotive

164. *Working replica of George Stephenson's* LOCOMOTION NO 1 *at Beamish, The North of England Open Air Museum.*

165. LOCOMOTIVE 'BRADDYLL' *at the Timothy Hackworth Victorian and Railway Museum.*

Works in 1840. An exact working replica of 'Locomotion' can be seen in action at Beamish the North of England Open Air Museum.

166. *The former* SHILDON WAGONWORKS.

167. STOCKTON AND DARLINGTON RAILWAY MARKER.

168. HOWNSGILL VIADUCT, *near Consett, built in 1858.*

169. BURN HALL *designed by Ignatius Bonomi and built between 1821-24.*

By 1901 the population of the area covered by the modern day administrative County had risen to 422,500. During the 19th century the building of mansions decreased but Lambton Castle near Chester-le-Street was erected between 1813-62 in mock mediaeval style. Ironically as the Lambtons were coal owners, the castle was built over an unsuspected coal pit and much of it had to be demolished. Ignatius Bonomi built Burn Hall south of Durham City between 1821-24 for the Salvin family and Eggleston Hall around 1820. Most buildings of the 19th century were public, such as the Assize Court in Durham City (1809-11 again by Bonomi), the Town Hall in Bishop Auckland (in the French style), and Ushaw (St.

170. LAMBTON CASTLE, *this mock castle was built around the core of Harraton Hall.*

Cuthbert's) College (in the Gothic style). The most remarkable building of the 19th century however is The Josephine and John Bowes Museum at Barnard Castle, which was built in the style of a French chateau to house the Bowes' art collections.

171. BISHOP AUCKLAND TOWN HALL, *Market Place, Bishop Auckland. Built in 1860-62 in the French style, it is now a multi-purpose library and arts centre.*

172. THE JOSEPHINE AND JOHN BOWES MUSEUM, *Barnard Castle*.

As within all economies in the twentieth century, there has been enormous change in the economy of County Durham. After the first World War world-wide recession led to a slump in the demand for coal. This was compounded by the development of diesel and petrol engines. At the same time many of the older collieries in the west and centre of the County were being worked out. After 1947 coal mining was mainly confined to the east of the County and the last mine to close was the Seaham Vane Tempest Colliery in 1994.

Having in many respects led the Industrial Revolution, County Durham found that it needed dramatically to modernise and diversify its industrial base through the introduction of new technologies and new skills. The scale of social and economic change has been staggering and has not been achieved without difficulty.

Huge problems were posed for local government which rose magnificently to the challenge. Over twenty square miles of industrial dereliction were reclaimed and it is difficult for today's visitors to believe that heavy industry once dominated this County. Some of the new industries attracted during the 1960s were branch plant operations which closed as companies retracted during a series of national recessions but important lessons were learned. Rationalisation has proceeded under careful management by the public sector, which has long been involved in economic regeneration measures. Durham County Council has led a wide-ranging economic development partnership, which includes the private sector, in a comprehensive and sustained strategy to regenerate the local economy. This has included important initiatives to nurture investment, support businesses, create fresh opportunities

173. RESTORED OPENCAST SITE, *Daisy Hill, near Sacriston.*

and raise the levels of skills. These measures now underpin the growing success of today's progressive economy which is becoming increasingly more robust, diverse and self-sustaining.

Above all, it is the character and entrepreneurial spirit of the people of the County together with the quality of the County's natural and historic environment and excellent geographical location which have ensured this remarkable transformation. The County is alive with a buzz of activity and the sounds of new industry and enterprise.

174. *Public art reflects the steelmaking and engineering heritage of the former Steelworks at Consett.*

CHAPTER 8

Living and Working in the County today

Today's County Durham lies at the heart of the North East Region, and is therefore an excellent business location, not only for access to the whole UK domestic market, but also to the many established and developing business and market opportunities in Europe. Those visiting the County soon realise just how much it has to offer and that it is a marvellous place in which to live, work and bring up a family.

The modern day administrative County of Durham is smaller than the historic County. Following reorganisations of local government, places on the Rivers Tyne and Wear, such as Gateshead, Jarrow and Sunderland, are now administratively separate from County Durham. Similarly, areas to the north of the River Tees, including Hartlepool and Stockton, are now part of the Teesside administration. More recently the Borough of Darlington became administratively independent. Recent surveys by local newspapers in all of these areas have, however, revealed that many people still identify strongly with the old County.

There is in County Durham a pleasant feeling of space as its population of 492,000 lives in an area covering 862 square miles

176. DURHAM CITY *by night*.

177. *Panoramic view of* CROOK TOWN CENTRE.

giving an average of 2.2 persons per hectare compared with 3.4 for England and Wales. There is room to move and settlements are well separated by attractive countryside. There are twelve main towns of which Durham City with a population of 37,700 is the largest. Consett and Stanley occupy high ground in the north west, and Chester-le-Street lies on the banks of Wear in the north of the County's central communications corridor. All of these are close to the large conurbation of Tyne and Wear. The port of Seaham on the east coast and the nearby new town of Peterlee are similarly close to Tyne and Wear. Durham City is located in the central corridor, while to the south lies another new town, Newton Aycliffe. To the west are Bishop Auckland, Spennymoor and Crook. Further inland, to the west in Teesdale, is the old market town of Barnard Castle, the gateway to the Pennine Dales.

A modern, comprehensive communications infrastructure has been established in the County linked to the excellent regional network, to the rest of the UK, to Europe and to Scandinavia. Roads are usually free from the traffic congestion experienced elsewhere. Through the County's central corridor, where most of its population lives, runs the East Coast main railway line and the A1 (M) which are arterial north-south routes connecting Scotland and the south of England. The fast internal road-links to the motorway ensure that the bulk of inland freight deliveries from the County's industrial estates can be made to the rest of the U.K. within 24 hours of despatch .

In addition to the County's own seaport at Seaham, which is well equipped to handle bulk and project cargoes, there is easy access to the port at Sunderland, the Port of Tyne, with all its modern cargo handling facilities, Teesport with the second largest deepwater port in the country, and Hartlepool, the third busiest port in the U.K. The excellence of the region's seaports is matched by the conveniently located airports at Newcastle and Teesside, both of which are within thirty minutes drive of Durham City, and offer scheduled flights to many European destinations. Regular scheduled flights form a connection with many British cities. Freight handling capacity and usage has risen rapidly and numerous specialist freight forwarding companies offer a full range of freight services.

The County has a well developed network of all types of industrial estates in a good choice of locations together with strategically located business parks and reserve sites for inward investors. It is not surprising that over one hundred companies from twenty countries such as the USA, Japan, France, Germany, Italy and Korea, including many whose names and

178. *New office accommodation at* THE IMEX CENTRE, *near Durham City.*

179. *With fast access to the country's north-south motorway,* AYCLIFFE INDUSTRIAL PARK *is home to over 250 companies.*

reputations are known world-wide, have recognised the benefits of County Durham as a business location and decided to locate their operations here. Together with the already well-established indigenous industries, these and new vigorous companies are ensuring the County continues to enjoy and develop an increasingly diversified and sophisticated economy. Particular strengths include key areas of science such as electronics, information technology, engineering, advanced materials, biotechnology and pharmaceuticals. Other important areas of production include plastic processing, the automotive industry, and food and drinks. Service industries too, are well represented.

County Durham has ample energy resources, including water from its own reservoirs and a supply from Kielder Reservoir in Northumberland, the largest man-made lake in Europe, and has access to plentiful supplies of North Sea Gas. New companies attracted to the

180. *Many world class companies have chosen to locate operations in County Durham. This site is at Spennymoor.*

County have been consistently pleased with their experience of the local workforce which is characterised by its skills, reliability and above all, flexibility and adaptability. Labour turnover

181. *In East Durham, where coal was once king,* MODERN BUSINESS PARKS *now provide homes for state-of-the-art call centre facilities.*

182. *County Durham is now home to many high-tech companies.*

183. *The County's economy includes an increasingly diverse range of industries.*

and absenteeism rates are regarded as extremely favourable and the area has always enjoyed a good reputation for its industrial relations.

184. *A wide range of precision engineering products are exported world-wide.*

There is a real sense of working together at every level, and industry is seen as an integral part of the community. Higher education institutes, which include the regional universities, work together in a joint initiative combining their resources in research, development and training in such a way as to ensure total collaboration and to provide an interface with industry and commerce to enable the full exploitation and utilisation of the immense intellectual and material resources available. Areas covered include computers in manufacturing, biotechnology and pharmaceuticals, energy and materials technology, electronics and analytical and design services. Science parks and other specialist facilities have also been established.

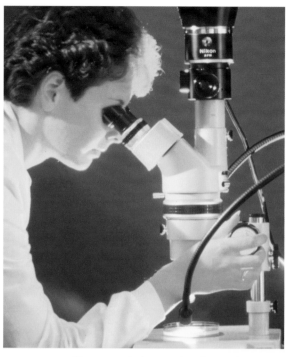

185. *Pharmaceutical research and manufacturing is based in the County.*

Within the Durham Dales in the west, which form a large part of the North Pennines Area of Outstanding Natural Beauty, and elsewhere in the centre and east, can be found the traditional

186. DRY STONE WALLING *in Weardale.*

agricultural, craft and cottage industries associated with a large rural county. The people of the County are proud of their natural and historic heritage and take great care to preserve its natural appeal.

187. TOW LAW AUCTION MART.

188. *Agricultural Shows are an important feature of life in rural Durham.*

189. STANHOPE SHOW.

190. *A winter walk on* THE WEARDALE WAY *near Wolsingham*.

191. *Sunset in* WEARDALE.

As a place to live, and to visit, both now and in the future, the County offers unsurpassed choice. Situated between the Lake District and the North Pennines to the west, and the beaches and limestone cliffs of its coastline with the North Sea beyond to the east, the County has some of the least spoiled countryside in Britain which includes spectacular landscape and memorable scenery.

192. *Sailing on* DERWENT RESERVOIR.

193. THE RIVER WEAR *at Finchale near Durham.*

194. GRETA BRIDGE *in Teesdale was rebuilt in 1773.*

195. LOW BARNS NATURE RESERVE *near Witton le Wear incorporates woods, lakes, ponds, riverside and meadows.*

Across the County, housing old and new blends with the dramatic contrasts in the landscape. Newcomers to the County have a great choice of locations in which to find their new home and develop a lifestyle to suit their needs. Whether their taste be for town houses, traditional country cottages, modern executive housing, cosy terraced cottages or well-planned modern estates, there is something to satisfy all tastes.

196. MODERN HOUSING *at Newton Aycliffe.*

197. VILLAGE HOMES *in Weardale.*

198. *Period houses in* BRANCEPETH VILLAGE *in mid Durham*.

199. *Peaceful village life can be found in places such as* MIDDLETON-IN-TEESDALE.

200. TOWN HOUSES, *Durham City*.

201. *A typical rural country cottage, here at* Romaldkirk, *in Teesdale*.

202. *There is a wide range of choice of modern executive housing.*

203. *A range of innovative ideas have been incorporated into new home design.*

204. *Modern terraced homes at Witton Gilbert.*

205. DURHAM SCHOOLS *provide a high level of education for students of all ages.*

206. THE UNIVERSITY OF DURHAM *is the third oldest in England.*

The County has an comprehensive network of over 300 schools, extensive nursery provision and colleges providing academic and vocational courses on a part-time and full-time basis. Durham University, with its excellent range of arts, science and social sciences departments, founded in 1832, is the third oldest in England and has an outstanding reputation for teaching and research.

207. ROMAN FORT, *Bishop Auckland.*
A Roman Legionary from the North Guard stands on the ancient Dere Street, the main road to the North, at Binchester.

The County's long history, its Christian and industrial heritage and its natural beauty have made it rich in places to see and things to do. A wide range of activities is available for resident and visitor alike. The past shapes the present and the County's proud past is everywhere stunningly displayed. For those interested in locations steeped in history and the romantic mysteries conjured by a turbulent past, places to be visited include Roman remains such as those at Binchester near Bishop Auckland, the largest Roman Fort in the County. Binchester lies on Dere Street, the Roman road from York to the Firth of Forth which became an important supply route for Hadrian's Wall. Today visitors can follow the Dere Street Trail along sections of the road almost 2,000 years old.

The County is dotted with impressive historic castles where the quality of their settings and the grandeur of their structures leaves the visitor breathless. Those in ruins present haunting images of the great events and times past.

208. Raby Castle.

209. *View from* DURHAM CATHEDRAL

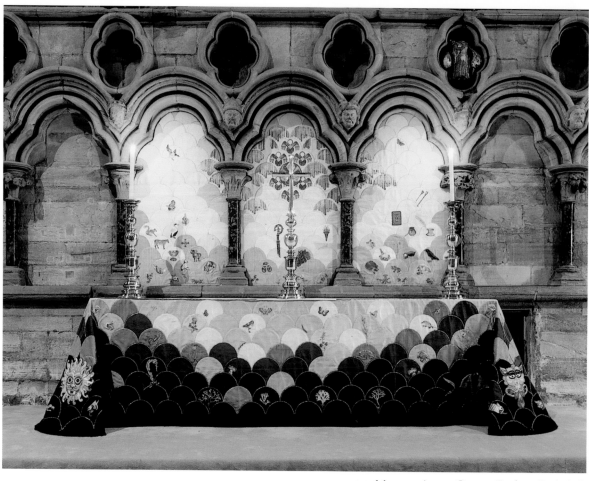

210. MODERN ALTAR CLOTH, *Durham Cathedral.*

At the heart of the County the imposing Norman Cathedral is one of the great architectural experiences of Europe. A visit to the hallowed interior of this living church cannot fail to move the spirit. Here can be seen the treasures of St. Cuthbert, including his pectoral cross, and beautifully illuminated manuscripts. The structure of the cathedral is itself a work of art with its great pillars and soaring vaults and stained glass windows. Elsewhere, the County is rich with other ancient and fascinating churches. St Helen's at St Helen Auckland is 12th century and unspoilt, and St. Edmund's at Sedgefield is mainly 13th century. The County boasts the oldest Methodist Chapel in continuous use - Newbiggin Methodist Chapel. High House Methodist Chapel at Ireshopeburn, now a museum, is also one of the earliest built.

The County's country houses and parklands have provided inspiration to many, including Sir Walter Scott, who used the palladian-style Rokeby Park as the setting for his ballad 'Rokeby'. At romantic Hardwick Hall Country Park the Hall is now an hotel. An area of 40 acres of 18th century parkland is being restored and features a serpentine lake and a classical temple.

For those who enjoy finding out about daily life in the past, many artefacts can be seen in the County's museums. At Beamish, the North of England Open Air Museum, one of the leading tourist attractions in the region, the visitor can

211. Beamish, The North of England Open Air Museum.

212. Beamish, The North of England Open Air Museum *is one of the County's great days out.*

213. THE GARAGE *at Beamish, the North of England Open Air Museum.*

experience miners' working conditions in a drift mine, climb into the winding house of a colliery or walk down a street complete with shops, a garage, a public house and other features which vividly reconstruct life in a north east town at the turn of the century. The origin of railways in the County is brought alive by the working replica of George Stephenson's Locomotion at Beamish; at the nearby Tanfield Railway visitors can take a steam-hauled ride on one of the oldest railways still in existence. The Timothy Hackworth Victorian and Railway Museum at Shildon displays some of the earliest examples of locomotives and railway infrastructure.

At the magnificent Josephine and John Bowes Museum in Teesdale, one of Britain's finest museums, can be seen the pre-eminent international art collection of John and his French wife, Josephine. The Museum proudly displays the wonderful cultural legacy left by the Bowes for the enjoyment of today's and future generations. The Museum's treasures include work by El Greco, Canaletto, and Gainsborough.

Visitors to the Museum can also marvel at the Silver Swan, an 18th century automaton, which is still operated every day, and view the grotesque two-headed calf. Archaeological and local history displays reveal some of the secrets of Durham's past.

214. THE JOSEPHINE AND JOHN BOWES MUSEUM, *Barnard Castle. Built in the style of the great French museums, it opened in 1892.*

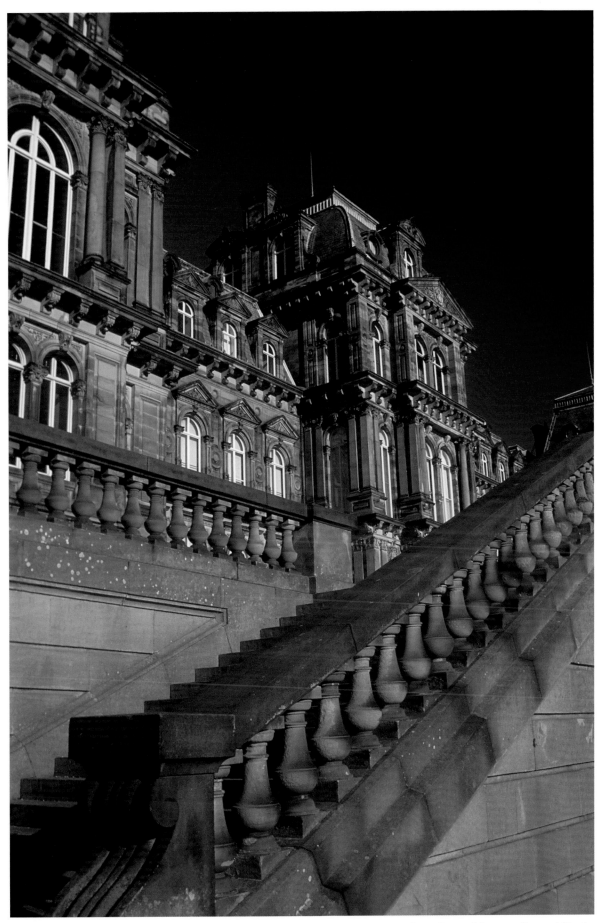

215. *The impressive stairway to* THE JOSEPHINE AND JOHN BOWES MUSEUM, *Barnard Castle*.

216. DURHAM LIGHT INFANTRY MUSEUM AND ART GALLERY, DURHAM CITY
*The Durham Light Infantry Museum displays the treasures of the Durham Light Infantry
and provides a changing programme of art and craft exhibitions.*

The Durham Light Infantry Museum tells the story of the fighting men of Durham. Men such as Adam Wakenshaw who won his Victoria Cross at Mersa Matruh in North Africa when, badly wounded, he continued to load and fire his anti-tank gun in a brave effort to stop the enemy advance. Men such as Jimmy Durham, the young Sudanese boy who was found by DLI soldiers on the banks of a river and brought up by them, serving first as a mascot and then as a soldier - one of the first black soldiers in a British Regiment. The Museum sets the story of the DLI in the context of life in County Durham, showing the strength of character of Durham people on active service and on the home front.

217. *The anti-tank gun on which Adam Wakenshaw won his posthumous VC is one of the Durham Light Infantry Museum's most popular visitor attractions.*

The County's industrial heritage is being brought alive in many ways to provide a fascinating and educational experience for all ages. Life for those employed in the early lead mining industry can be experienced at Killhope Lead Mining Centre where the great water wheel can be seen turning today. Here visitors can also journey underground into Park Level Mine, see the processes by which lead was extracted and see what living conditions were like for the North Pennine lead miners and their families. This multi-award-winning site provides an experience of 'history you can touch' and a great day out for all the family.

218. KILLHOPE LEAD MINING CENTRE, WEARDALE.

219. *The lead mining story is vividly brought to life at* KILLHOPE LEAD MINING CENTRE.

Sporting enthusiasts can savour the many pleasures available, which include a visit to the home of the County's First Class Cricket Club at Chester-le-Street, or a game of golf at one of the County's 18 golf courses. Other facilities include multi-court squash complexes, sailing and water-skiing, fast-water canoeing, climbing, shooting, and riding to name but a few. There are 31 recreational and leisure centres spread around the County, and many private sports clubs. Football is a way of life in County Durham and teams such as Bishop Auckland, Crook, and Tow Law have enjoyed cup success.

220. *Aerial view of the new home for County Durham's* FIRST CLASS CRICKET *Team at Chester-le-Street*.

221. RACING AT SEDGEFIELD *attracts many visitors to the County*.

222. GOLF IN FRONT OF LUMLEY CASTLE, *Chester-le-Street*.

223. WITTON CASTLE HORSE TRIALS.

For those who prefer more gentle forms of leisure activity the choices range from cycling and walking to salmon and trout fishing in picturesque locations. Over 50 miles of the County's former railway lines which originally linked colliery villages have now been

224. FISHING AT TUNSTALL RESERVOIR, *near Wolsingham*.

converted into a network of footpaths and bridleways for walking and cycling. Much of the County's peaceful country scenery can therefore be enjoyed without the necessity of driving and without exposure to traffic. Much has been done to develop picnic sites in scenic areas, such as those near the Deerness, Derwent and Lanchester Valley Walks, and these have a great appeal for families. The County's rivers provide opportunity for peaceful riverside walks through spectacular surroundings. Even during peak visitor periods the sheer expanse of open countryside guarantees peace and quiet whether the visitor's preference be for open fells, rolling countryside or shady woodland. The County's tranquil reservoirs make ideal places to get away from everyday cares and worries.

225. *Walking in* WEARDALE.

226. WALKING IN TEESDALE.

227. *Cycling along* FOREST DRIVE, HAMSTERLEY FOREST.

228. GUIDED WALKS *are a popular pastime in County Durham for residents and visitors.*

Theatrical tastes are provided for with the Royal Shakespeare Company seasons in Newcastle. The North has its own orchestra, the Northern Sinfonia, and venues around the County host such events as stage plays, operas, musicals, ballet and pop concerts. There are several art galleries and the rich mixture of cultural entertainment provides something to suit everyone's taste.

Life in the County today is enriched by a range of cultural activities based firmly in the region's heritage. Brass band concerts are a popular entertainment and standards of playing are very high. Folk music is enjoyed throughout the County and songs performed include those of great Durham songwriters such as Tommy Armstrong and Alexander Barrass. Artists such as Norman Cornish and Tom McGuiness have established an international reputation for their portraits of Durham life and scenes, and the late Sid Chaplin's plays and short stories provide a window on Durham life.

229. Music in the open air has long been a popular entertainment in Durham. THE BANDSTAND ON THE RACECOURSE *enjoys spectacular views of the historic City.*

Traditional crafts, such as making proggy mats and quilt-making, are still practised and enjoyed by new generations. The creativity of traditional crafts people is acknowledged by important collections in local museums. The Durham Miners' Gala continues to be a spectacular and hugely colourful annual event attended by thousands of people when banners representing miners' lodges and union branches are paraded.

230. *The annual* MINERS' GALA *attracts thousands of visitors.*

231. MINERS' GALA, *Durham City.*

232. HAND THROWN POTTERY, *Sedgefield.*

233. BISHOP AUCKLAND *is a major market town.*

There are modern shopping centres, and in Durham City pedestrian precincts wind their way through the cobbled streets and allow the visitor the best of both worlds. Here is quiet shopping amongst the historic buildings, with the Castle and Cathedral as a backdrop and the River Wear meandering its way around the City. After shopping and sightseeing, a relaxing boat ride can be enjoyed around the great horseshoe meander which embraces the rock from which the great cathedral looks down.

234. *Walkers can enjoy an early morning view of* THE CORN MILL AND PREBENDS BRIDGE, *Durham City.*

235. THE MARKET PLACE, *Durham City.*

236. *Aerial view of the* HEART OF DURHAM CITY *showing the Cathedral in its magnificent 'World Heritage' setting.*

237. THE PRINCE BISHOP RIVER CRUISER, *on the River Wear.*

238. BOATING ON THE RIVER WEAR *is a popular past-time for residents and visitors*.

239. TRAINING FOR THE ANNUAL DURHAM REGATTA *-the second oldest regatta in the country and a popular event in Durham's tourist calendar.*

240.

241. *The past provides a perspective for the future.*

County Durham provides all the essential ingredients, and more, for a full and highly satisfying lifestyle. With great care, the people of Durham have produced all the conditions necessary for a modern lifestyle and modern economy, but have managed to preserve the beauty of the County. The towns and countryside together offer a stimulating and varied environment for anyone who wishes to make their home in County Durham. This County, with nearly two millennia of recorded history and 10,000 years of evidence of human occupation, is proud of its heritage and its achievements.

The County's well established links with Europe show that the County is forward-looking. Together with its splendid history, this foresight and preparedness gives County Durham the foundation needed to go on with great anticipation, and confidence that it will make its mark during the third millennium A.D.

CHAPTER PHOTOGRAPHS

ACKNOWLEDGEMENTS

The County Council would like to thank Ken Frankish, the Director of Economic Development and Planning and County Council staff, particularly, Harry Elliott, Jennifer Gill, Malcome Howe, Ian Stewart and Iain Watson, for their assistance in the preparation of the book and all others who provided advice, information, comments and photographs.

The County Council would also like to thank Frank Manders for his considerable contribution in reviewing the historical content of the book.

All of the photographs apart from those listed below belong to the County Council.

The following photographers have made significant contributions from their private collections:

Colin Burt – 26, 27, 30, 36, 38, 39, 42, 72, 121, 174, 176, 177, 197.

Philip Nixon – 3, 8, 31, 40, 44, 45, 56, 61, 93, 105, 118, 130, 135, 138, 146, 154, 156-159, 162, 164, 165, 167, 168, 175, 186-189, 192, 199, 201, 207, 213, 219, 223, 226, 228, 232, 233, 237.

Graeme Peacock – 5, 6, 9, 17, 20, 32, 37, 53, 67, 73, 74, 76, 82, 83, 85, 86, 89, 90, 92, 110, 112, 115, 132, 143, 171, 209, 240.

Eddie Ryle-Hodges – 2, 7, 10, 11, 14, 15, 16, 19, 21, 29, 64, 79, 106, 108, 124, 133, 136, 152, 153, 155, 172, 173.

Darin Smith – 12, 18, 22-24, 33-35, 41, 43, 46-50, 52, 54, 55, 66, 68, 87, 91, 98, 100, 103, 107, 109, 113, 114, 119, 122, 125, 126, 128, 134, 139, 140-142, 190, 191, 193, 195, 198, 208, 211, 215, 221, 224, 225, 227, 238.

Doug Whittaker – 13, 28, 78, 79, 81, 84, 97, 102, 104, 137, 149, 210, 229, 230, 231, 234, 235, 239, 241.

The following are also thanked for supplying photographic material:

Airfotos – 236.

John Baxter – 214.

Beamish, The North of England Open Air Museum – 212.

County Durham Development Company – 161, 179-185

The Dean and Chapter of Durham – 75, 77, 94, 95.

English Nature – 51.

University of Durham and Royston Thomas – 88, University of Durham – 206.